The Central Intelligence Agency

The Central Intelligence Agency

Rafaela Ellis

CHELSEA HOUSE PUBLISHERS

Editor-in-Chief: Nancy Toff
Executive Editor: Remmel T. Nunn
Managing Editor: Karyn Gullen Browne
Copy Chief: Juliann Barbato
Picture Editor: Adrian G. Allen
Art Director: Giannella Garrett
Manufacturing Manager: Gerald Levine

Staff for THE CENTRAL INTELLIGENCE AGENCY:

Senior Editor: Elizabeth L. Mauro
Associate Editor: Pierre Hauser
Copyeditor: Gillian Bucky
Production Coordinator: Laura McCormick
Picture Research: Martin Baldessari
Designer: Noreen M. Lamb
Layout: Foulk Purvis Design

Creative Director: Harold Steinberg

3 5 7 9 8 6 4 2

Library of Congress Cataloging-in-Publication Data

Ellis, Rafaela
    The Central Intelligence Agency.

    (Know your government)
    Bibliography: p.
    Includes index.
    1. Intelligence service—United States—History. 2. United States. Central
Intelligence Agency. [1. Intelligence service. 2. United States. Central
Intelligence Agency. 3. United States—Foreign relations—1945- . 4. Spies] I.
Title. II. Series: Know your government
JK468.I6E837   1987   327.1'2'06073

ISBN 0-87754-831-5

Cover photographs: Examples of the advanced technology the Central
Intelligence Agency (CIA) uses to gather intelligence information. Satellite
dishes (bottom left) intercept communications signals, electronic monitors (top)
aid surveillance efforts, and high-flying aircraft (bottom right) carry cameras to
photograph foreign military installations.

Frontispiece: A telephone bugging device.

CONTENTS

KNOW YOUR GOVERNMENT

CHELSEA HOUSE PUBLISHERS

Government: Crises of Confidence

Arthur M. Schlesinger, jr.

From the start, Americans have regarded their government with a mixture of reliance and mistrust. The men who founded the republic did not doubt the indispensability of government. "If men were angels," observed the 51st Federalist Paper, "no government would be necessary." But men are not angels. Since human beings are subject to wicked as well as to noble impulses, government was deemed essential to assure freedom and order.

At the same time, the American revolutionaries knew that government could also become a source of injury and oppression. The men who gathered in Philadelphia in 1787 to write the Constitution therefore had two purposes in mind. They wanted to establish a strong central authority and to limit that central authority's capacity to abuse its power.

To prevent the abuse of power, the founding fathers wrote two basic principles into the new Constitution. The principle of federalism divided power between the state governments and the central authority. The principle of the separation of powers subdivided the central authority itself into three branches—the executive, the legislative, and the judiciary—so that "each may be a check on the other." The *Know Your Government* series focuses on the major executive departments and agencies in these branches of the federal government.

The Constitution did not plan the executive branch in any detail. After vesting the executive power in the president, it assumed the existence of "executive departments" without specifying what these departments should be. Congress began defining their functions in 1789 by creating the Departments of State, Treasury, and War. The secretaries in charge of these departments made up President Washington's first cabinet. Congress also provided for a legal officer, and President Washington soon invited the attorney general, as he was called, to attend cabinet meetings. As need required, Congress created more executive departments.

Setting up the cabinet was only the first step in organizing the American state. With almost no guidance from the Constitution, President Washington, seconded by Alexander Hamilton, his brilliant secretary of the treasury, equipped the infant republic with a working administrative structure. The Federalists believed in both executive energy and executive accountability and set high standards for public appointments. The Jeffersonian opposition had less faith in strong government and preferred local government to the central authority. But when Jefferson himself became president in 1801, although he set out to change the direction of policy, he found no reason to alter the framework the Federalists had erected.

By 1801 there were about 3,000 federal civilian employees in a nation of a little more than 5 million people. Growth in territory and population steadily enlarged national responsibilities. Thirty years later, when Jackson was president, there were more than 11,000 government workers in a nation of 13 million.

8

The federal establishment was increasing at a faster rate than the population.

Jackson's presidency brought significant changes in the federal service. He believed that the executive branch contained too many officials who saw their jobs as "species of property" and as "a means of promoting individual interest." Against the idea of a permanent service based on life tenure, Jackson argued for the periodic redistribution of federal offices, contending that this was the democratic way and that official duties could be made "so plain and simple that men of intelligence may readily qualify themselves for their performance." He called this policy rotation-in-office. His opponents called it the spoils system.

In fact, partisan legend exaggerated the extent of Jackson's removals. More than 80 percent of federal officeholders retained their jobs. Jackson discharged no larger a proportion of government workers than Jefferson had done a generation earlier. But the rise in these years of mass political parties gave federal patronage new importance as a means of building the party and of rewarding activists. Jackson's successors were less restrained in the distribution of spoils. As the federal establishment grew—to nearly 40,000 by 1861—the politicization of the public service excited increasing concern.

After the Civil War the spoils system became a major political issue. High-minded men condemned it as the root of all political evil. The spoilsmen, said the British commentator James Bryce, "have distorted and depraved the mechanism of politics." Patronage, by giving jobs to unqualified, incompetent, and dishonest persons, lowered the standards of public service and nourished corrupt political machines. Office-seekers pursued presidents and cabinet secretaries without mercy. "Patronage," said Ulysses S. Grant after his presidency, "is the bane of the presidential office." "Every time I appoint someone to office," said another political leader, "I make a hundred enemies and one ingrate." George William Curtis, the president of the National Civil Service Reform League, summed up the indictment. He said,

> The theory which perverts public trusts into party spoils, making public employment dependent upon personal favor and not on proved merit, necessarily ruins the self-respect of public employees, destroys the function of party in a republic, prostitutes elections into a desperate strife for personal profit, and degrades the national character by lowering the moral tone and standard of the country.

The object of civil service reform was to promote efficiency and honesty in the public service and to bring about the ethical regeneration of public life. Over bitter opposition from politicians, the reformers in 1883 passed the Pendleton Act, establishing a bipartisan Civil Service Commission, competitive examinations, and appointment on merit. The Pendleton Act also gave the president authority to extend by executive order the number of "classified" jobs—that is, jobs subject to the merit system. The act applied initially only to about 14,000 of the more than 100,000 federal positions. But by the end of the 19th century 40 percent of federal jobs had moved into the classified category.

Civil service reform was in part a response to the growing complexity of American life. As society grew more organized and problems more technical, official duties were no longer so plain and simple that any person of intelligence could perform them. In public service, as in other areas, the all-round man was yielding ground to the expert, the amateur to the professional. The excesses of the spoils system thus provoked the counter-ideal of scientific public administration, separate from politics and, as far as possible, insulated against it.

The cult of the expert, however, had its own excesses. The idea that administration could be divorced from policy was an illusion. And in the realm of policy, the expert, however much segregated from partisan politics, can never attain perfect objectivity. He remains the prisoner of his own set of values. It is these values rather than technical expertise that determine fundamental judgments of public policy. To turn over such judgments to experts, moreover, would be to abandon democracy itself; for in a democracy final decisions must be made by the people and their elected representatives. "The business of the expert," the British political scientist Harold Laski rightly said, "is to be on tap and not on top."

Politics, however, were deeply ingrained in American folkways. This meant intermittent tension between the presidential government, elected every four years by the people, and the permanent government, which saw presidents come and go while it went on forever. Sometimes the permanent government knew better than its political masters; sometimes it opposed or sabotaged valuable new initiatives. In the end a strong president with effective cabinet secretaries could make the permanent government responsive to presidential purpose, but it was often an exasperating struggle.

The struggle within the executive branch was less important, however, than the growing impatience with bureaucracy in society as a whole. The 20th century saw a considerable expansion of the federal establishment. The Great Depression and the New Deal led the national government to take on a variety of new responsibilities. The New Deal extended the federal regulatory apparatus. By 1940, in a nation of 130 million people, the number of federal workers for the first time passed the 1 million mark. The Second World War brought federal civilian employment to 3.8 million in 1945. With peace, the federal establishment declined to around 2 million by 1950. Then growth resumed, reaching 2.8 million by the 1980s.

The New Deal years saw rising criticism of "big government" and "bureaucracy." Businessmen resented federal regu-

11

lation. Conservatives worried about the impact of paternalistic government on individual self-reliance, on community responsibility, and on economic and personal freedom. The nation in effect renewed the old debate between Hamilton and Jefferson in the early republic, although with an ironic exchange of positions. For the Hamiltonian constituency, the "rich and well-born," once the advocate of affirmative government, now condemned government intervention, while the Jeffersonian constituency, the plain people, once the advocate of a weak central government and of states' rights, now favored government intervention.

In the 1980s, with the presidency of Ronald Reagan, the debate has burst out with unusual intensity. According to conservatives, government intervention abridges liberty, stifles enterprise, and is inefficient, wasteful, and arbitrary. It disturbs the harmony of the self-adjusting market and creates worse troubles than it solves. Get government off our backs, according to the popular cliché, and our problems will solve themselves. When government is necessary, let it be at the local level, close to the people. Above all, stop the inexorable growth of the federal government.

In fact, for all the talk about the "swollen" and "bloated" bureaucracy, the federal establishment has not been growing as inexorably as many Americans seem to believe. In 1949, it consisted of 2.1 million people. Thirty years later, while the country had grown by 70 million, the federal force had grown only by 750,000. Federal workers were a smaller percentage of the population in 1985 than they were in 1955—or in 1940. The federal establishment, in short, has not kept pace with population growth. Moreover, national defense and the postal service account for 60 percent of federal employment.

Why then the widespread idea about the remorseless growth of government? It is partly because in the 1960s the national government assumed new and intrusive functions:

12

affirmative action in civil rights, environmental protection, safety and health in the workplace, community organization, legal aid to the poor. Although this enlargement of the federal regulatory role was accompanied by marked growth in the size of government on all levels, the expansion has taken place primarily in state and local government. Whereas the federal force increased by only 27 percent in the 30 years after 1950, the state and local government force increased by an astonishing 212 percent.

Despite the statistics, the conviction flourishes in some minds that the national government is a steadily growing behemoth swallowing up the liberties of the people. The foes of Washington prefer local government, feeling it is closer to the people and therefore allegedly more responsive to popular needs. Obviously there is a great deal to be said for settling local questions locally. But local government is characteristically the government of the locally powerful. Historically, the way the locally powerless have won their human and constitutional rights has often been through appeal to the national government. The national government has vindicated racial justice against local bigotry, defended the Bill of Rights against local vigilantism, and protected natural resources against local greed. It has civilized industry and secured the rights of labor organizations. Had the states' rights creed prevailed, there would perhaps still be slavery in the United States.

The national authority, far from diminishing the individual, has given most Americans more personal dignity and liberty than ever before. The individual freedoms destroyed by the increase in national authority have been in the main the freedom to deny black Americans their rights as citizens; the freedom to put small children to work in mills and immigrants in sweatshops; the freedom to pay starvation wages, require barbarous working hours, and permit squalid working conditions; the freedom to deceive in the sale of goods and securities; the

13

freedom to pollute the environment—all freedoms that, one supposes, a civilized nation can readily do without.

"Statements are made," said President John F. Kennedy in 1963, "labelling the Federal Government an outsider, an intruder, an adversary.... The United States Government is not a stranger or not an enemy. It is the people of fifty states joining in a national effort.... Only a great national effort by a great people working together can explore the mysteries of space, harvest the products at the bottom of the ocean, and mobilize the human, natural, and material resources of our lands."

So an old debate continues. However, Americans are of two minds. When pollsters ask large, spacious questions—Do you think government has become too involved in your lives? Do you think government should stop regulating business?—a sizable majority opposes big government. But when asked specific questions about the practical work of government—Do you favor social security? unemployment compensation? Medicare? health and safety standards in factories? environmental protection? government guarantee of jobs for everyone seeking employment? price and wage controls when inflation threatens?—a sizable majority approves of intervention.

In general, Americans do not want less government. What they want is more efficient government. They want government to do a better job. For a time in the 1970s, with Vietnam and Watergate, Americans lost confidence in the national government. In 1964, more than three-quarters of those polled had thought the national government could be trusted to do right most of the time. By 1980 only one-quarter was prepared to offer such trust. But by 1984 trust in the federal government to manage national affairs had climbed back to 45 percent.

Bureaucracy is a term of abuse. But it is impossible to run any large organization, whether public or private, without a bureaucracy's division of labor and hierarchy of authority. And we live in a world of large organizations. Without bureaucracy modern society would collapse. The problem is not to abolish bureaucracy, but to make it flexible, efficient, and capable of innovation.

Two hundred years after the drafting of the Constitution, Americans still regard government with a mixture of reliance and mistrust—a good combination. Mistrust is the best way to keep government reliable. Informed criticism is the means of correcting governmental inefficiency, incompetence, and arbitrariness; that is, of best enabling government to play its essential role. For without government, we cannot attain the goals of the founding fathers. Without an understanding of government, we cannot have the informed criticism that makes government do the job right. It is the duty of every American citizen to *Know Your Government*—which is what this series is all about.

Nathan Hale, shown here shadowing a British soldier, was one of many spies who served in the colonial army.

ONE

The Art of Espionage

Espionage—the practice of spying—has a long history as a survival tool of rulers and nations. The earliest written reference to spying occurs in the Bible's "Book of Numbers," when the Lord told Moses to "spy out the land of Canaan . . . and the people that dwelleth therein." In the 5th century B.C., Chinese rulers used spies to infiltrate enemy camps, and 13th-century Mongol emperor Kublai Khan sent agents into Europe long before most Europeans had even heard of Mongolia. In the West, government espionage can be traced to 16th-century England, when Queen Elizabeth I used spies to uncover political enemies within her own court.

Today, almost every major world power has a government branch dedicated to gathering foreign intelligence (information about other nations) so that its leaders will be aware of any threats to its security. Great Britain has its MI6 and the Soviet Union uses the KGB. In the United States, the Central Intelligence Agency, or CIA, performs intelligence functions.

The Need for the CIA

The CIA was created after World War II, when a congressional committee examined the Japanese bombing of Pearl Harbor. The investigation revealed that the United States could have anticipated the attack if all the available information had been compiled and analyzed. Congress decided that, in addition to the traditional military and political intelligence gathering, the United States needed a central group to coordinate information about foreign countries. In 1947, Congress passed the National Security Act, and the CIA was born.

Since its creation, the CIA has become the backbone of the world's largest intelligence community. Almost a dozen other agencies help the CIA perform its job of collecting, evaluating, and distributing information. CIA officers travel throughout the world—usually "under cover"—gathering data about the military, political, economic, scientific, technical, and sociological conditions in other nations and monitoring those nations' own agents.

Then the agency furnishes all of this data to the president and other high-level officials so they can make informed decisions about U.S. foreign policy. For example, economic data may help legislators decide how much foreign aid they should grant, and political intelligence (information about the motives and attitudes of foreign governments) can help the president decide which foreign ambassadors he should receive.

National security often hinges on adequate intelligence. For example, negotiators need accurate intelligence on Soviet weapons for arms limitation talks. And military leaders use information on foreign troop movements to help protect the United States and other countries from attack. In fact, military intelligence has been vital to the nation's survival since its beginning.

Early American Intelligence

Until the CIA's creation, the United States had no permanent, peacetime intelligence unit. But, throughout the country's history, its leaders had employed intelligence techniques during times of war. The first American use of espionage occurred in the 1700s, when the colonists were preparing for war with their British rulers. The Continental Congress (the colonial legislature that served as the American government prior to the adoption of the Constitution) secretly employed spies and authorized paramilitary missions against British installations.

After the American Revolution began, General George Washington used spies to monitor British troop movements. Alexander Hamilton was one of America's earliest cryptographers, creating codes for Washington's secret military correspondence. The country's first espionage hero was a 21-year-old teacher named Nathan Hale. A lieutenant in the Continental army, Hale volunteered to penetrate British-occupied New York City by disguising himself as a civilian. The British army caught him spying near what is now midtown Manhattan. Just before he was hanged for his activities, he uttered these famous last words: "I only regret that I have but one life to lose for my country."

After Hale's death, Washington established an intelligence bureau under Major Benjamin Tallmadge and instructed his men to "mix as much as possible among the [British] officers and . . . visit the Coffee Houses, and all public places" to gather information. Washington's war ledger shows that the Continental Congress allotted him almost $17,000 for this intelligence activity during the revolution.

The United States did not need espionage again until its Civil War. In the early 1860s, President Abraham Lincoln hired the famous private investigator Allan Pinkerton to provide information on the size and strength of Confederate forces. Some experts believe that the very inaccuracy of Pinkerton's information helped the Union win the war—he so greatly overestimated Confederate strength that Union generals always readied twice as many troops as needed.

George Washington, shown here with his generals, created America's first intelligence bureau during the revolutionary war.

During the Civil War, Abraham Lincoln confers in a Union army camp with private investigator Allen Pinkerton (left).

After Pinkerton resigned as the Union's chief spy, President Lincoln placed Major George Sharpe in charge of a new military intelligence group. Sharpe recruited volunteers to spy for General Ulysses S. Grant, leader of the Union army (and later president of the United States). Some of the best information Grant received came from a black servant who, while working at the home of Confederate President Jefferson Davis, eavesdropped on conversations between the Rebel leader and his staff.

After the Civil War ended, America's leaders recognized the need for a more organized method of gathering information. As the United States became increasingly involved in world politics, the government more closely examined its intelligence needs. In the late 1800s, the U.S. military founded America's first official intelligence agencies.

In 1889, the House of Representatives (pictured here) and the Senate appropriated funds for the newly formed intelligence branches of the army and the navy.

TWO

Forerunners of the CIA

In 1882, the U.S. Navy created the first official American espionage service, the Office of Naval Intelligence (ONI). In 1885, the army established its own intelligence branch, known as the Military Information Division (MID). Each had a function specific to its service branch: ONI gathered information on the naval strength of foreign nations, and MID assembled data on foreign armies. In 1889, Congress appropriated money for these intelligence groups, which had previously been financed by the military. Congressional funding represented the first public recognition of America's intelligence needs.

In 1898, the Spanish-American War tested the newly formed agencies. Although the MID and the ONI had some success during the war, they were limited by the narrow scope of their investigations. The agencies learned much about the enemy's military strategy but discovered little about their diplomatic or political strategies.

Allied troops in their trenches during World War I. After the United States entered the war in 1917, the army established intelligence unit MI-8 to examine foreign mail.

Less than 20 years later, when the United States became embroiled in World War I, a young State Department employee named Herbert O. Yardley recognized the need for a more comprehensive intelligence program. He convinced the army to establish a secret information group to intercept and decipher foreign mail in an attempt to root out enemy agents. The group, known as MI-8, was a forerunner of today's CIA.

MI-8's methods were rudimentary by today's standards. Operatives gained most of their information by seizing letters before they reached their destination and analyzing them for secrets—literally, by reading other people's mail. Yet Yardley and his team of cryptologists caught a number of German spies by uncovering and decoding hundreds of messages—many written in invisible ink—hidden in foreign correspondence.

When World War I ended, in November 1918, the army no longer saw a need for the services of MI-8. But Yardley was convinced that the United States needed a permanent intelligence service to examine foreign diplomatic correspondence and create secret codes for the nation's own diplomatic mail. In 1919 he persuaded the Departments of War and State to put him in charge of America's first nonmilitary intelligence agency, known as the Black Chamber.

The existence of Yardley's intelligence group was a closely guarded secret—many of the government's top officials had no idea that the Black Chamber had been formed. Throughout the 1920s, the Black Chamber cracked the secret codes of friendly and hostile nations alike. For example, it deciphered Japan's diplomatic code before a naval disarmament conference in 1921. The information gained from Japanese correspondence allowed American negotiators to base their conference strategy on inside information about Japan's naval strength. By 1928 the Black Chamber had broken the diplomatic codes of Great Britain, France, Germany, and the Soviet Union and was regularly sending coded cor-

Delegates at the 1921 international disarmament conference. America based its conference strategy on data gathered by the Black Chamber, the nation's first nonmilitary intelligence agency.

Henry L. Stimson disbanded the Black Chamber after he became secretary of state in 1929.

respondence to ambassadors, military leaders, and other U.S. representatives around the globe.

The Black Chamber continued its activities until 1929, when newly inaugurated President Herbert Hoover appointed Henry L. Stimson as his secretary of state. Outraged to learn that a government organization was reading private diplomatic correspondence, Stimson immediately dismantled the Black Chamber, stating, "Gentlemen do not read each other's mail." Yardley was dismissed, and America once again had no centralized information service. For the next several years the only intelligence reaching the U.S. government came from military attachés, ambassadors, and other Americans stationed oversees, or from the intelligence arms of the military.

"Wild Bill" Donovan

In the mid-1930s, as mounting tensions in Europe foreshadowed World War II, President Franklin Delano Roosevelt recognized the need for a comprehensive intelligence effort. Alarmed at the sketchy information he was receiving from American contacts in Europe, Roosevelt called upon World War I hero and noted lawyer William Joseph Donovan to investigate.

Donovan had won a Congressional Medal of Honor and earned the nickname "Wild Bill" for his exploits as the leader of the "Fighting 69th" Infantry during World War I. (The story goes that Donovan was berating his troops for their sluggish performance in battle when one of his soldiers yelled out, "Well, I guess we're just not as wild as you, Bill!") At Roosevelt's request, Donovan spent most of the 1930s traveling to foreign capitals and meeting with political leaders. Each time he returned to the United States, Donovan briefed Roosevelt on what he had learned. Although he publicly referred to his journeys as business

In the 1930s, William Donovan traveled to Europe on intelligence-gathering "business trips."

trips, most of the leaders he met knew he was gathering information for President Roosevelt. French and British officials welcomed Donovan's visits because they hoped his information would convince Roosevelt to grant their countries military and economic assistance.

After the European nations became involved in World War II, Roosevelt discussed with Donovan the possibility of a new U.S. intelligence agency. On July 11, 1941, the president established the office of the Coordinator of Information (COI) and named Donovan as its director. The COI's purpose was to "collect and analyze all information and data which may bear upon national security, and . . . make the same available to the President and such departments and officials of the Government as the President may determine."

As soon as the COI's establishment was announced, a roar of protest arose in Washington. The powerful director of the Federal Bureau of Investigation (FBI), J. Edgar Hoover, felt that the COI was usurping his role as America's chief investigator. The State Department, which had a special intelligence unit in Latin America, also feared that the new agency would undercut its authority. Many senators worried that the COI would allow the White House to spy on political enemies and dissenters within the United States, and Major General George V. Strong, head of army intelligence, feared that Donovan's leadership role would conflict with his own.

Despite this dissent, President Roosevelt approved the COI's first budget in November 1941; he even appointed his son James as Donovan's assistant. Donovan immediately began organizing his agency.

Less than a month after his budget was approved, Donovan was attending a New York Giants football game when a voice came over the loudspeaker summoning him to the telephone. James Roosevelt was calling to inform him that the Japanese had bombed Pearl Harbor. The United States was now at war.

Japan's attack on Pearl Harbor brought the United States into World War II, which altered U.S. intelligence operations.

The Office of Strategic Services

American involvement in World War II immediately altered the nature of the COI's office. It entwined military and diplomatic intelligence concerns and forced the COI to work closely with the armed services. In June 1942, Congress redesignated the COI as the Office of Strategic Services (OSS), reporting to the Joint Chiefs of Staff (a committee composed of the armed services' leaders) rather than the president.

OSS chief Donovan had his work cut out for him in 1942. Germany's intelligence machine, the *Abwehr,* was already operating in Europe. Fortunately, the OSS received aid from Britain's diplomatic and military intelligence groups, known respectively as SIS (Secret Intelligence Service) and MI6. British agents instructed Americans in the use of early warning radar systems, coastal defenses, and other tricks of the espionage trade.

During World War II, Roosevelt (left) and Churchill met to share information on the Axis gathered by their respective nation's intelligence agencies.

Throughout the war, British and American intelligence operations worked together closely. Donovan collaborated with William Stephenson, a British security chief stationed in the United States, and President Roosevelt and British Prime Minister Winston Churchill shared the vital information that their intelligence teams gathered.

The OSS was organized into nine branches, each with a separate responsibility. OSS employees stationed in the United States worked in four branches: Research and Analysis, Morale Operations, Schools and Training, and Foreign Nationalities. These groups trained recruits for foreign missions and collected and analyzed political, economic, and military data on enemy nations. They also wrote and produced literature and radio broadcasts encouraging opposition to the Axis powers of Germany, Italy, and Japan.

The most secret OSS divisions—Secret Intelligence, Special Operations, Counterintelligence, Operational Groups, and the

Maritime Unit—conducted espionage in the midst of the war zone. Officers stole into enemy territory in attempts to blow up bridges and military installations, infiltrate enemy organizations, and even assassinate political and military figures.

The OSS was extremely successful in fighting the Axis powers. By 1943 it had infiltrated and stolen secrets from Adolf Hitler's German High Command in Berlin and sent guerrilla teams to assist Albanians and Yugoslavians fighting the occupying German army. It had also broadcast anti-Axis propaganda from clandestine radio stations in Sicily and mainland Italy and paved the way for the Allied invasion of North Africa by reporting Axis advances there. Because of these actions, Hitler ordered his commanders to execute on the spot any prisoner suspected of being an OSS officer.

To fill the needs of its specialized departments, the OSS hired people from every walk of life. It recruited scholars, teach-

During the later stages of the war, OSS officers infiltrated the German High Command, shown here at a 1942 meeting.

31

OSS officers parachuted into Axis-occupied territory to gather strategic information and to sabotage enemy installations.

ers, mechanics, artists, policemen, lawyers, and businesspeople. Unknown to the public, some of America's most familiar personalities participated in secret wartime missions. Actor Sterling Hayden sailed on OSS missions to German-occupied Albania, and Notre Dame University football star Joe Savoldi parachuted into Italy for the OSS.

Foreign civilians helped the OSS in its less dangerous operations. Its youngest operative was a British boy, aged 12, who was fluent in several languages. The boy overheard the conversations of a group of suspected Axis spies and translated them for the agency. Thanks to the boy's eavesdropping, the OSS captured an entire spy ring; they rewarded him with an $8 stamp-collecting album.

The OSS was so effective that as early as 1944, President Roosevelt considered establishing a postwar intelligence agency. He even asked William Donovan to draft a memo on the subject. Before the president could present the idea publicly, however, an angry J. Edgar Hoover leaked Donovan's memo to the press. This caused a furor among conservative congressmen on Capitol Hill and forced the president to delay decision on the agency.

In 1945, after Roosevelt's death and the end of World War II, President Harry S. Truman—under increasing pressure from Congress and the FBI—disbanded the OSS. Intelligence gathering again became a function controlled by the Departments of War and State, and "Wild Bill" Donovan went back to his Wall Street law practice.

President Truman signs the National Security Act, which established the CIA, the nation's first permanent peacetime intelligence agency.

THREE

The CIA's
Early Years

In the euphoric atmosphere after World War II, most Americans welcomed President Truman's decision to disband the OSS. After all, the United States had always dismantled its intelligence apparatus in times of peace. Soon, however, the nation turned a wary eye toward a wartime ally, the Soviet Union. Under Josef Stalin's leadership, the Soviets began expanding their influence in Eastern Europe, and Americans started to wonder if their nation was heading toward another Pearl Harbor.

While trying to gain accurate information about Soviet military and espionage activities, Truman encountered the same problems Roosevelt had faced a decade earlier. Individual intelligence sources submitted conflicting and muddled information, making it impossible for him to make informed strategic decisions. Truman, who only a year earlier had disbanded the OSS, decided that America needed a permanent, peacetime intelligence agency.

In 1947, Congress examined Truman's request for a centralized intelligence service. Opponents again raised many of the same objections that they had brought up when Roosevelt had tried to form the COI. The FBI greatly resented the plan, and J. Edgar Hoover again voiced strong objections. Many senators feared that an intelligence service could be misused to act as the president's private army or to spy on U.S. citizens. To help dispel these fears, Truman sent high-ranking cabinet members to testify before Congress. One of the most notable was Navy Secretary James Forrestal, who assured Congress that the proposed intelligence authority would limit its investigations "to purposes outside of this country."

Forrestal and other officials convinced Congress, and the intelligence resolution passed both houses. On September 18, Truman signed it into law as the National Security Act of 1947. The act had three important provisions. It established the National Security Council (NSC) to oversee all U.S. intelligence operations, created the position of director of central intelligence (DCI) to manage intelligence activities, and—most important—founded the CIA.

The National Security Act stated the CIA's purposes: to correlate and evaluate intelligence and distribute it to appropriate officials; to advise the NSC on matters of national security; to recommend ways to coordinate the various intelligence departments' activities; to carry out "services of common concern"; and to "perform such other functions and duties related to intelligence affecting the national security as the NSC will from time to time direct."

To allay Hoover's vocal criticism, the act prohibited the CIA from participating in domestic operations, placing all investigative activity within the United States firmly under FBI control. The act also created a number of oversight boards to ensure that the CIA acted within the limits of its charter.

Open for Business

On September 18, 1947, under the leadership of its first DCI, Rear Admiral Roscoe H. Hillenkoetter, the CIA began operations. Hillenkoetter believed that Congress intended for the CIA only to organize information gathered by other intelligence agencies, not to collect it. Consequently, the agency spent most of its first few years coordinating intelligence gathered by other sources and creating foreign affairs reports for the president and the NSC.

The CIA maintained a low profile until June 1950, when Communist North Korea invaded South Korea. The United States, which had sent troops to Korea in 1945 and had withdrawn them in 1949, was unprepared for this turn of events. Because the CIA had not predicted the timing of the attack (al-

Rear Admiral Roscoe H. Hillenkoetter, the first director of central intelligence, believed the CIA should organize intelligence, not collect it.

though some staffers had suggested the possibility of an invasion), many accused the agency of failing to perform its duty. As a result, the CIA underwent a period of internal reorganization. In October 1950, Rear Admiral Hillenkoetter was replaced by General Walter Bedell Smith, a well-respected World War II commander and a former ambassador to the Soviet Union.

The new director rehired a number of top OSS officers and placed them in charge of new CIA departments. Most significantly, the CIA began to devote most of its time, money, and employees to clandestine intelligence operations. It established covert (secret) information offices around the globe, and by 1952, it had more than 3,000 overseas employees. The demand for information created by the Korean conflict forced the agency to grow rapidly. By 1953 the CIA—which had not even existed six years earlier—employed more than 10,000 people in the United States and abroad.

The Dulles Years

In February 1953, recently inaugurated President Dwight D. Eisenhower appointed Allen Dulles as director of central intelligence. Under Dulles's direction, the agency enjoyed a period of immense popularity with the public. As fear of communism escalated with the cold war, Americans came to view the CIA as the nation's best defense against the Soviet threat. This viewpoint was fostered by CIA activities that led to the installation of the shah of Iran's pro-American regime in 1953 and the ouster of Guatemala's leftist government in 1954. The goal of these activities was to stabilize particularly troubled areas and to develop relations with leaders in those areas to ensure that they did not fall under Soviet influence.

One of the CIA's first major operations was helping to restore the shah of Iran to his throne in 1953.

Allen Dulles (left), who built the CIA's reputation in the 1950s, pictured with his brother, Secretary of State John Foster Dulles.

In addition to these successes, the agency benefited from the public's fascination with Dulles himself. A noted lawyer and brother of then-Secretary of State John Foster Dulles, he began his intelligence career in the OSS. Charming and sophisticated, he embodied the "James Bond" spy image that was popular during the 1950s.

Dulles secured his popularity in 1954, during the infamous McCarthy hearings on Communist influences in government. When Senator Joseph McCarthy charged that Communists had infiltrated the CIA, Dulles openly challenged him to prove it. McCarthy soon withdrew the claim. Dulles's bold confrontation with a man few dared to challenge helped enhance the agency's image.

Dulles's CIA concentrated on creating new methods of gathering intelligence. In 1953 it hired Lockheed Aircraft Corporation to design a plane for reconnaissance (observation to gather information). The result was the U-2 spy plane, the most advanced craft of its day. The light, high-flying U-2 could take clear photographs from as high as 15 miles (24 kilometers) above the earth.

The plane was a boon for the agency, and soon the CIA hired young pilots to fly the plane secretly over the Soviet Union to monitor its secret buildup of military installations. In 1960, the Soviets shot down a U-2 piloted by American Francis Gary Powers. President Eisenhower at first denied that the mission had

In 1960, Soviet premier Nikita Khrushchev (center) examines equipment from the American U-2 plane shot down over his country.

taken place, but eventually stated his belief that the United States was obliged to learn all it could about Soviet military strength. The incident further enhanced the CIA's reputation as a stalwart defender of democratic freedom.

The Bay of Pigs and Beyond

America's honeymoon with the CIA ended abruptly on April 17, 1961, when a group of Cuban exiles—trained and armed by the CIA—invaded Cuba's Bay of Pigs. They intended to overthrow Communist Premier Fidel Castro, who was orchestrating a military buildup. The plan, created by the CIA during Eisenhower's term and put into action with President John F. Kennedy's approval, failed dismally. Castro's military crushed the small fighting force of 1,400 men, and U.S. involvement in the operation was immediately exposed.

Worldwide reaction to the Bay of Pigs incident was swift and angry. In the United States, public opinion turned against the CIA. As a result, President Kennedy restructured the agency. In November 1961, he replaced Dulles with John A. McCone, the former head of the Atomic Energy Commission. Kennedy instructed the new DCI to "assure the proper coordination, correlation, and evaluation of intelligence from all sources." In other words, he returned the CIA's emphasis to evaluating intelligence rather than conducting paramilitary operations.

McCone believed that the agency needed to further develop its technology. He created the Directorate for Science and Technology to concentrate on improving photographic operations and signals intelligence (information gained by intercepting electronic communications). In 1962, McCone used photographic reconnaissance to discover Soviet missile sites in Cuba. Many consider this discovery one of the CIA's greatest triumphs. It led to the Cuban Missile Crisis, which ended when President Kennedy blockaded Cuba and forced the Soviets to withdraw the missiles.

President Johnson congratulates William Raborn on his appointment as CIA director. Criticism of the agency marred Raborn's term.

Although the Cuban success redeemed the agency somewhat, the CIA suffered another period of strife in 1965 when McCone left the agency after a dispute with President Lyndon Johnson over the agency's involvement in Vietnam, where it was working to install and support a non-Communist government in the face of Communist destabilization attempts. In McCone's place, the president appointed retired naval officer William "Red" Raborn.

43

Raborn had no intelligence experience, and his term was difficult. On the day Raborn was sworn in as CIA chief, President Johnson sent the marines into the Dominican Republic to quell violence there. Unprepared for the sudden intelligence needs this created, Raborn spent several months answering criticism over his handling of the affair. Raborn also had difficulty coordinating the intelligence effort in Vietnam, where the United States had installed military advisors. President Johnson quickly lost confidence in him and replaced him in 1966 with Richard Helms, a CIA veteran who had begun his intelligence career in the OSS.

Vietnam and Watergate

Richard Helms's tenure as head of the CIA was turbulent. When American involvement in Vietnam escalated into the Vietnam War, the American public's opposition increased, along with its

The CIA's involvement in the Vietnam War caused public opinion to turn against the agency in the late 1960s.

suspicion of the agency's role in the conflict. Beginning in the late 1960s, a number of revelations in the American press seemed to justify that suspicion. Reports suggested that the CIA had been involved in foreign assassination plots, surveillance of antiwar protesters, and other actions that seemed to go beyond the agency's mandate. Public sentiment against the agency grew more and more hostile.

In 1972, the public learned that two people who had broken into the Democratic headquarters in the Watergate Hotel—the event that led to President Richard M. Nixon's resignation— were former CIA employees. The public also learned that CIA Deputy Director Robert Cushman had provided one of the burglars, former CIA staffer E. Howard Hunt, with a wig and disguise. However, investigations later revealed that the CIA had played a minimal role in the Watergate scandal.

In February 1973, President Nixon replaced Helms with James Schlesinger. The new chief held office for only six months before Nixon transferred him to the Defense Department during a departmental reorganization. In July 1973, William Colby, a longtime CIA man, was sworn in as director of central intelligence.

Marchers protest the Vietnam War. Charges that the CIA had illegally infiltrated the antiwar movement rocked the agency.

FOUR

Investigation
and Change

Before William Colby became
the CIA's director, he had helped Schlesinger draft a memo to
agency employees instructing them to report any information
they had about illegal or unethical CIA activities. The resulting
list, the "Family Jewels," detailed hundreds of illegal or questionable operations that the CIA had performed since its beginning.

The Family Jewels list, which Colby claimed would help prevent future violations, was intended for agency employees only.
But some of the information eventually leaked to the press. In
December 1974, the *New York Times* reported that "well-placed
government sources" had admitted that the CIA had conducted
"massive" illegal espionage activities, including the use of wire-
taps, break-ins, mail intercepts, and surveillance, to investigate
American citizens in an attempt to monitor allegedly anti-Ameri-
can activities. The accusations created a firestorm of protest
against the agency. A public that had never quite forgotten the
Bay of Pigs fiasco began clamoring for an investigation.

The Rockefeller Commission

On January 6, 1975, President Gerald R. Ford created the Commission on CIA Activities Within the United States to examine charges of domestic spying. The eight-member commission, chaired by Vice-President Nelson A. Rockefeller, included such notables as former Secretary of Commerce John T. Conner and ex-governor of California Ronald Reagan. Known as the Rockefeller Commission, this panel spent five months interviewing CIA employees and others about agency operations.

A 1975 meeting of the Rockefeller Commission, a panel created to examine CIA domestic activities.

The commission found that, whereas "the great majority" of the CIA's operations complied with the law, many "were plainly unlawful." It reported that the agency had violated a provision of the 1947 National Security Act that strictly forbade it from conducting domestic espionage.

The list of illegal activities included break-ins at the homes of 12 former or current CIA employees and experiments with mind-controlling drugs that had resulted in at least one death. The commission also found that for more than 20 years the agency had conducted an illegal mail interception program. From 1952 until 1973, the CIA had intercepted thousands of pieces of correspondence traveling from the Soviet Union and other Communist countries to the United States. It either photographed the outside of envelopes (an operation known as mail cover, performed to record who sent or received foreign correspondence) or actually opened mail and read or photographed its contents.

The most shocking revelation, however, was Operation CHAOS, which began in the 1960s. In this operation, CIA activities included surveillance and bugging of five American journalists and infiltration and surveillance of several antiwar protest groups. The commission found that the agency had kept files on more than 7,500 American citizens and had paid college students to gather information on leaders of some student protest groups.

In addition to revealing these clearly illegal actions, the commission discovered that Operation CHAOS had been initiated on President Johnson's specific orders and continued to function at President Nixon's request. However, the commission's report declared that all illegal domestic operations had ended in 1974, and that by 1975 the agency was operating according to its charter.

President Ford hoped that the Rockefeller Commission's findings would end all suspicion of the CIA. He was wrong. Many people thought the commission had whitewashed the CIA's activities in order to stem public outrage. As a result, both houses of Congress formed their own investigative committees.

The Rockefeller Commission revealed that President Nixon, shown resigning in 1974, had condoned certain illegal CIA actions.

The Church and Pike Committees

In early 1975, Senator Frank Church of Idaho established the Senate Select Committee to Study Governmental Operations with Respect to Intelligence Activities. Unlike the Rockefeller Commission, which had investigated only domestic CIA operations, the Senate committee decided to examine all intelligence activities. Soon, the House of Representatives also convened a committee to investigate all intelligence activities—the House Select Committee on Intelligence, chaired by Representative Otis Pike of New York.

For 15 months, these councils—known as the Church and Pike committees—held hearings on the workings of the CIA, the FBI, and other intelligence agencies. They called scores of agency employees and ex-employees to testify. DCI Colby later wrote that he spent two or three days each week for almost two years appearing before one committee or the other.

Both committees agreed with the Rockefeller Commission's findings that the CIA had violated its charter by engaging in domestic operations. Further, they concluded that the agency had also participated in a number of illegal or unethical foreign operations in its attempts to curtail Soviet influence. These operations included plotting the assassinations of foreign leaders (such as Cuba's Fidel Castro, the Dominican Republic's Rafael Trujillo, and Zaire's Patrice Lumumba), creating political strife in Chile

William Colby spent a large part of his two-year term as CIA director testifying before Congress about illegal agency activities.

that led to President Salvador Allende's assassination, and illegally providing weapons to foreign rebel movements. The committees also discovered that agency scientists had stockpiled poisonous snake venom and had produced a gun that could shoot poison darts. (The agency claimed that it had never used either the weapon or the poison.)

The Senate and House concluded that these abuses occurred largely because Congress had neglected its duty to oversee the CIA. The committees declared that the agency needed stronger congressional supervision. After considering the committees' findings, President Ford replaced Colby with George Bush, the former U.S. ambassador to the United Nations. Then,

Frank Church, chairman of a Senate committee investigating the CIA, displays a poison dart gun produced by the agency.

George Bush became CIA director as part of President Ford's attempt to reform the agency after the Pike and Church reports.

on February 18, 1976, Ford issued an order reorganizing the CIA and providing for stronger supervision of the agency.

Ford's directive, Executive Order 11905, addressed many of the problems cited by the committees. It specifically forbade participation in political assassination and restricted intelligence collection techniques. The order also gave more power to the NSC and established the Intelligence Oversight Board (IOB) to review all questionable agency activities. The era of unchecked CIA operations had presumably ended.

The Carter Years

When Jimmy Carter campaigned for the presidency in 1976, CIA reform was an important part of his platform. After his election, Carter enacted measures to further restrict and supervise the CIA. He replaced George Bush with Admiral Stansfield Turner and instructed the new DCI to ensure that the agency engaged in no illegal activities. Turner removed more than 800 officers and drastically reduced covert action as the agency concentrated on technical operations, such as satellite photography and signals intelligence.

Carter's presidency marked a period of transition for American attitudes toward government. Slowly, as the country began to recover from the traumas of Watergate and Vietnam, the anti-CIA sentiment of the early 1970s began to wane. A series of events at home and abroad spurred this change in public attitude.

After succeeding Ford as president, Jimmy Carter continued his predecessor's reorganization of the CIA.

Ayatollah Khomeini's overthrow of the shah of Iran in 1979 led many Americans to question whether Presidents Ford and Carter had gone too far in restricting the CIA's powers.

In 1978, two young Californians who worked for a CIA contractor sold technological secrets to the Soviet Union. (The movie *The Falcon and the Snowman* later recounted their story.) In the following year, Iranian militants toppled the shah of Iran's CIA-installed government. Then, on November 3, 1979, supporters of the Ayatollah Khomeini, the leader of Iran's Islamic Revolution, took more than 50 U.S. embassy employees hostage.

These three events reshaped the national mood. People started questioning whether CIA reform had gone too far and was now preventing the agency from effectively protecting national security. Many blamed President Carter for the agency's ineffectiveness. During the 1980 presidential race between Carter and challenger Ronald Reagan, the weakened CIA became a central issue.

The CIA Under Reagan and Casey

In January 1981, Reagan became the 40th president of the United States. Keeping his campaign promise of strengthening the CIA, he replaced DCI Turner with William Casey, a lawyer who had headed the OSS's London office during World War II. Reagan assigned Casey the task of revitalizing the CIA, and in order to help restore the agency's power, Reagan made the DCI part of his cabinet.

In the years following his appointment, Casey increased the agency's staff by more than 2,500. He created new positions and rehired most of the 800 officers who had been released during

William Casey, appointed CIA director in 1981, was given free reign by President Reagan to revitalize the agency.

the Carter years. To help house this staff, he approved construction of a 1,000,000-square-foot (90,000-square-meter) addition to the agency's headquarters in Langley, Virginia. Casey also increased covert operations by stepping up secret intelligence and paramilitary operations in unstable areas of interest to the Soviets, such as Afghanistan, Angola, Lebanon, and Nicaragua.

Public sentiment added to Casey's power. In an era of terrorist bombings and hijackings, many Americans felt the CIA needed to grow stronger in order to prevent such occurrences. The rash of cases involving Americans spying for the Soviet Union and other countries also seemed to evidence a need for the United States to step up its own operations. Even Congress, which less than a decade before had censured the CIA strongly, began to change its opinion. At Casey's urging, Congress appropriated 25 percent more money for intelligence, bringing the CIA's budget to more than $3 billion per year. By 1986, intelligence constituted one of the fastest-growing portions of the federal budget.

The CIA enjoyed relative freedom in its operations until early 1987, when it once again became embroiled in controversy. Congress began investigating whether the agency had provided funds and logistical support to the Contras, revolutionary forces in Nicaragua, at a time when a Congressional law forbade such aid. Congress also examined whether the CIA had helped to divert to the Contras money acquired by members of the Reagan administration through secret arms sales to Iran. To complicate matters further, Casey was hospitalized for removal of a malignant brain tumor as hearings on the Iran-Contra scandal began, and in May 1987 he died without having testified.

The CIA has faced many changes and controversies since its establishment in 1947. But throughout the years, it has served as the ear of the United States, providing the nation with information to help it manage its foreign relations and monitoring potential threats to its security.

Most of the CIA's estimated 16,000 employees work at the agency's headquarters in Langley, Virginia.

FIVE

The Intelligence Community

The National Security Act of 1947 placed the CIA at the hub of an information network known as the intelligence community. Today, twelve agencies constitute that community: the CIA; the FBI; the National Reconnaissance Office; the National Security Agency; the Defense Intelligence Agency; the intelligence corps of the army, navy, and air force; the Drug Enforcement Administration; and the intelligence divisions of the Departments of State, Energy, and the Treasury. Each agency gathers information in its area of expertise and gives it to the CIA, which coordinates and analyzes the data. The CIA uses this data to create reports, which it then distributes to the proper authorities.

The National Security Act also outlined the chain of command for the CIA and the intelligence community. Although subsequent legislation redefined the agency's scope and limitations, its basic structure and organization still conform to the provisions of this act.

The Intelligence Community

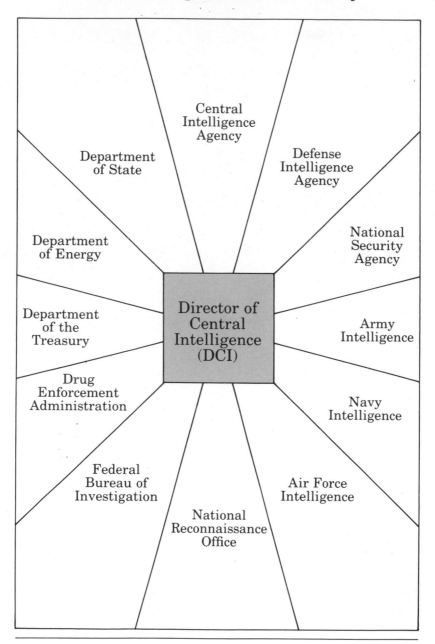

Central
Intelligence
Agency

Department
of State

Defense
Intelligence
Agency

Department
of Energy

National
Security
Agency

Director of
Central
Intelligence
(DCI)

Department
of the
Treasury

Army
Intelligence

Drug
Enforcement
Administration

Navy
Intelligence

Federal
Bureau of
Investigation

Air Force
Intelligence

National
Reconnaissance
Office

The DCI's Role

The leader of the CIA, called the director of central intelligence (DCI), is appointed by the president with the Senate's advice and consent. As head of the CIA, the DCI controls the agency's day-to-day operations, makes decisions on activities and procedures, appoints deputies and other staff members, and represents the agency to the intelligence community, the NSC, and the president. The directors of the other intelligence agencies perform similar functions.

The DCI does more than just direct the CIA, however. He also coordinates all U.S. intelligence activities. Although he has no direct authority over the other intelligence agencies, the DCI organizes their activities to ensure that they do not duplicate one another's efforts or work toward conflicting goals. As coordina-

Under President Reagan, the director of the CIA attended high level policy meetings, such as the one shown here.

tor, the DCI also chairs the National Foreign Intelligence Board (NFIB), a group composed of all of the intelligence agencies' leaders. He consults with NFIB members to formulate goals and policies for the entire intelligence community.

Based on the CIA's mandate to coordinate, analyze, and distribute information, the DCI also produces national intelligence. As the agency's leader, the DCI is ultimately responsible for producing reports on intelligence findings. Each morning, he delivers a briefing book to the White House that details important findings and predicts future events.

Inside the CIA

In addition to the DCI, the president also appoints a deputy director of central intelligence, or DDCI. The DDCI acts as the DCI's second-in-command and takes full responsibility for the agency when the DCI is absent, ill, or incapacitated.

The DCI and DDCI receive support from the Resource Management Staff and the National Intelligence Tasking Center. The Resource Management Staff assists the DCI with programming and budget concerns. The National Intelligence Tasking Center—a small group of experts in such fields as strategic weaponry, economics, the Soviet Union, and Latin America— analyzes data and informs the DCI of the most pressing issues facing the CIA.

The nuts and bolts of the CIA are its four directorates— Administration, Science and Technology, Operations, and Intelligence. A deputy director appointed by the DCI heads each directorate.

The Directorate of Administration runs the agency's day-to-day operations. It handles personnel, data processing, finance, medical services, and employee training. One of its most important functions is protecting the security of CIA personnel, facilities, and information from infiltration or discovery by enemy

Direction, Supervision, and Coordination of National Intelligence

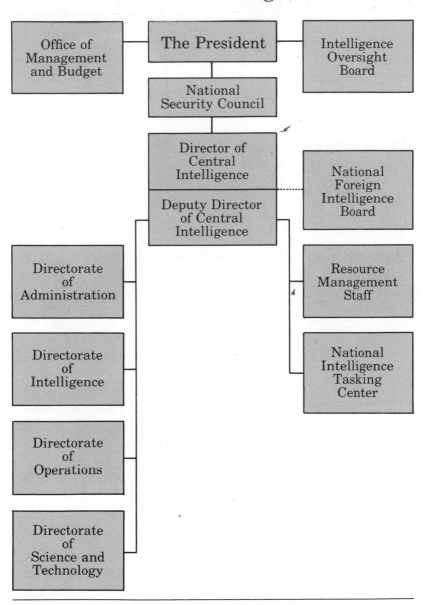

*At the CIA's operations center in Virginia, workers feed into
computers information gathered by officers around the world.*

agents. This function, called counterintelligence, includes a variety of techniques: conducting security checks on agency employees and their families and acquaintances, guarding CIA facilities with security cameras and other equipment, and even spying on foreign spies, suspected spies, and foreign embassies and officials.

The Directorate of Science and Technology informs the agency of the latest scientific and technological advances, supplies technical and scientific information to the CIA's other departments, and develops devices for officers to use in the field. Details about the directorate's work are closely guarded, but it employs some of the nation's most brilliant scientific researchers.

The CIA's most secretive branch is the Directorate of Operations. It performs the agency's covert maneuvers, including clandestine collection of intelligence and covert paramilitary operations. Little is known about its activities, but because of their sometimes gritty nature, it has been nicknamed the "Department of Dirty Tricks."

The analytical branch of the CIA is the Directorate of Intelligence. This directorate evaluates all the information gathered by the intelligence community and generates reports, called intelligence estimates. The intelligence directorate employs experts in hundreds of fields, ranging from military strategy to Eastern philosophy.

The People of the CIA

The actual number of CIA employees is classified information, but experts estimate that the agency employs more than 16,000 people to collect, analyze, and produce intelligence. Linguists, economists, historians, nuclear scientists, industrial engineers, lawyers, psychologists, chemists, agriculturalists, physicians, and experts in such specialized fields as Chinese boatbuilding and Asian religions all work in the national intelligence effort.

Although the only absolute requirement for CIA employees is U.S. citizenship, the agency sets exacting criteria for its recruits. In fact, about 80 percent of all CIA job applicants never even get as far as an interview. The agency screens them out immediately because of a lack of education or what it terms an "unfavorable" background. Of the approximately 20 percent remaining, the CIA refuses more than half because investigations reveal that they have trouble keeping secrets or have relatives in Communist countries who could make them subject to foreign pressure.

Those who make it past this stage—about five percent of all applicants—must take a lie detector test to determine if they

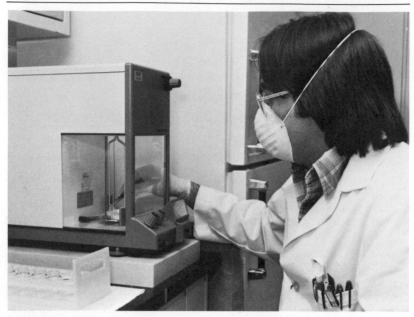

The CIA employs experts in a variety of scientific fields to analyze data and to create new technology for the agency.

have engaged in acts the agency considers undesirable (such as revealing secret information). All applicants who pass this stage undergo a complete physical examination. Candidates who wish to be officers must enter a rigorous physical training program similar to that of military boot camp.

At the end of this screening process, the agency accepts only 1 percent of all applicants. Yet despite the grueling application process, more than 150,000 people apply for CIA jobs every year.

Most CIA employees are "white," or overt, employees. Although they cannot disclose the nature of their work to anyone, many of them are allowed to acknowledge that they work for the agency. Most overt employees work at CIA headquarters in Langley, Virginia, although some are stationed in foreign countries.

The most talked-about CIA workers are the "black," or covert, employees, engaged in the CIA's dangerous undercover operations. They not only must deny working for the CIA, they usually deny their own names, adopting new identities complete with new families, educations, and backgrounds. Although covert employees constitute less than five percent of CIA personnel, the information they gather is vital to the intelligence effort.

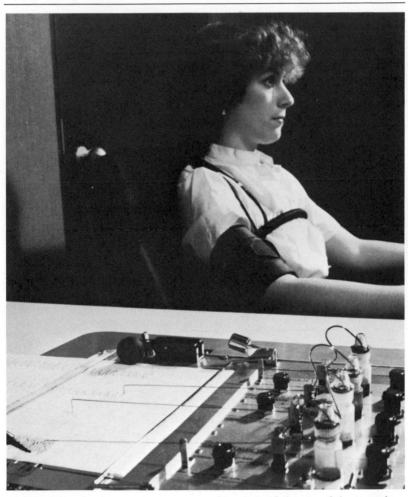

A woman undergoes a lie detector test, part of the careful screening process by which the CIA evaluates potential employees.

Guidance and Oversight

The CIA—and indeed, all of the intelligence community's bureaus—answer to the president. In fact, the president's foreign policy priorities directly determine the CIA's policies and actions. But in a nation founded on the principle of checks and balances, even the president cannot have absolute power over intelligence. To prevent an unsupervised intelligence service from violating civil rights, a number of executive and legislative agencies oversee intelligence activities.

The most important oversight board is the National Security Council, or NSC. The president, the secretaries of state and defense, and a presidential military advisor constitute the NSC,

President Reagan presides over a meeting of the National Security Council, one of several government agencies that oversee the CIA.

which surveys all U.S. intelligence activities and directly supervises the DCI. The NSC mechanism was designed to serve two purposes: to make the CIA accountable to the nation's highest officers and to ensure that the president's top advisors have access to the intelligence they need to make decisions.

Another executive-level watchdog group is the Intelligence Oversight Board (IOB). It reviews all intelligence activities and is required to report any improper or illegal activities to the president. The board consists of three presidential appointees from the private sector.

In addition to the NSC and IOB supervision at the executive level, congressional subcommittees also oversee the CIA. Designated members of the House and Senate Armed Services and Appropriations committees meet with the DCI to examine foreign intelligence programs and analyze budget requests. In recent years, Congress has watched the agency more closely and has demanded more details of CIA operations. In 1986, the Senate requested an itemized strategy plan outlining the CIA's priorities for the coming decade. Although such a request would have been unthinkable only a decade ago, the agency complied.

Funding the CIA

Each year, the president presents an itemized budget to Congress, outlining how much money each government agency will need during the following year. However, unlike that of all other agencies, the CIA's budget is not listed in detail. Because of the secret nature of most of the agency's work, its budget is classified—the CIA does not publicly record how much money it needs for its projects.

To protect the CIA's confidentiality, the government appropriates money to other departments and transfers it to the CIA later. Most of the CIA's money funnels through the Department of Defense, and it also receives money from the State Department. Although this system makes it impossible for the average citizen to know exactly how much of each tax dollar funds the CIA, estimates value the agency's budget at more than $3 billion a year. The budget is so highly classified that only 15 senators and 16 representatives, members of intelligence oversight committees, know how much money the CIA gets and how it uses the funds.

The Office of Management and Budget (OMB) examines the CIA's budget demands before they are presented to the congressional watchdogs. In this process, the OMB, which coordinates the budget requests of each government department, seeks to ensure that the CIA's requests accurately reflect its needs.

The CIA and the Public

Since the disclosures of the 1970s, the CIA has become more open in dealing with the public. Today, the agency even has a special department, the Office of Public Affairs, whose sole purpose is to answer public inquiries about agency activities. Americans may write or call this office to request unclassified information on CIA activities and findings.

Each year, the CIA declassifies more than 100 reports and produces scores of bulletins, maps, charts, and reviews that individuals can purchase for a small fee. Three government agencies publish and disseminate unclassified CIA data: the Government Printing Office, the Library of Congress, and the National Technical Information Service. Anyone who wishes to buy such diverse CIA publications as the *World Factbook*, the *International Energy Statistical Review*, or the *USSR Agricultural Atlas* can write to these agencies for a list of available titles.

Since 1966, the Freedom of Information Act (FOIA) has required U.S. government agencies to make many of their records available to the public upon request. Records exempted from disclosure include those involving national security and trade secrets. The FOIA was supplemented by the Privacy Act of 1974, which requires federal agencies to provide individuals with copies of any files compiled about them or groups with which they are affiliated. Of course, limits exist on what will be supplied. For example, internal personnel records, interagency mail, and records compiled for law enforcement purposes will not be released. The CIA can also refuse a request for information if the response would jeopardize national security.

Unlike the fictional James Bond, portrayed here by Sean Connery, CIA officers spend more time researching than chasing villains.

SIX

The Intelligence Process

CIA staffers like to tell a story about former DCI Richard Helms. One night in 1965, President Lyndon Johnson invited Helms to his ranch in Texas for dinner. Among the other invited guests was Senator Eugene McCarthy of Minnesota, a vocal critic of the CIA. While the guests were dining, the senator began to question Helms.

First, McCarthy asked Helms if he could identify the wine they were drinking. Helms responded that he could not. Then, McCarthy asked him if he knew the names of the flowers in the table's centerpiece. Again, Helms had no answer. McCarthy smiled wryly and said, "James Bond would have known the answers."

CIA officers like that story because it proves something they want people to know—the real CIA bears little resemblance to glamorous movie images of spies and spying. Unlike James Bond and other fictional characters, real intelligence officers must invest many hours in research and analysis to uncover the infor-

Eugene McCarthy, a senator from Minnesota from 1958 to 1970, was a vocal critic of the CIA.

mation vital to national security. And national security rarely hinges on an officer's knowledge of wine or flowers.

In many ways, the CIA works like a business, matching a consumer with a product. The CIA's consumers are the president, the NSC, and select members of Congress. Its product is information pertaining to U.S. national security. The agency's work so closely resembles a corporation's that its employees call it "the company."

Producing Intelligence

Intelligence production involves four steps. The first is determining what sort of information must be gathered to meet consumer needs. The DCI and the National Foreign Intelligence Board (NFIB) make this determination—the intelligence requirement—

in consultation with the president and the NSC. The president and the NSC tell the DCI what information they need, and each NFIB member tells the DCI whether his agency has the information currently available.

If the information is not available, the DCI determines the agency best equipped to uncover it. (For example, if the requested data concerns foreign naval strength, he may decide that the navy's intelligence service should assess the situation.) This decision is the second step—the resource allocation requirement.

The Intelligence Process

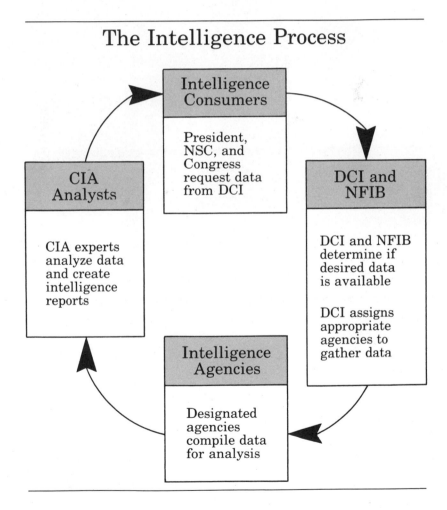

Intelligence Consumers

President, NSC, and Congress request data from DCI

DCI and NFIB

DCI and NFIB determine if desired data is available

DCI assigns appropriate agencies to gather data

Intelligence Agencies

Designated agencies compile data for analysis

CIA Analysts

CIA experts analyze data and create intelligence reports

Once the DCI selects an agency, the chosen agency investigates and compiles the data. This step is called collection management. After information has been gathered, the agency sends it to the CIA's headquarters in Langley, Virginia, for analysis by a team of experts.

CIA analysts, specialists from a variety of fields, combine all the information gathered on a subject—the "raw" intelligence—and create a report, bulletin, or survey. The analysts' releases, called estimates, are the intelligence product, the final step in the intelligence process. The intelligence product takes many forms. One important form is the *National Intelligence Daily*, the most highly classified newspaper in the nation. Only about 60 people, including the president, the NSC, and the intelligence community chiefs, receive the *Daily*. It presents the most pressing intelligence problems and the latest findings.

Collecting Intelligence

Each year, the CIA processes millions of facts on thousands of subjects. CIA staff members research and verify each piece of information using a variety of collection methods. They gather some information covertly and some overtly.

The CIA gets a lot of its overt information simply by asking. The agency interviews foreigners who visit the United States and "debriefs" business travelers, journalists, and others who travel abroad. The agency has offices in more than 40 U.S. cities. Employees at these branch offices receive a wealth of information from local businesspeople and scholars who have contacts in, or frequently travel to, foreign countries. Citizens who think they may have useful information for the agency can contact these field offices, which are listed in local telephone directories.

Another overt collection method is monitoring the foreign press. CIA employees review foreign radio and television broadcasts for the news and opinions in other lands. They also buy millions of publications from other nations. Agency linguists then translate this material, which includes everything from roadmaps and train schedules to novels, small-town newspapers, and popular magazines. Other members of the CIA staff enter all of this foreign literature into huge computers to make it available to any agent who needs it.

Overt sources offer the agency a safe and relatively inexpensive way to gather nonsecret yet important information about daily life in other parts of the world. The CIA collects the majority of its information—a full 80 percent—through these methods. But another 20 percent of the agency's information requires more dangerous and expensive collection techniques. In some

The front page of Pravda, *the official Soviet daily, one of hundreds of foreign newspapers that CIA linguists examine each day.*

Photographic intelligence, one of the CIA's three main types of covert intelligence, produced this picture of Soviet missiles in Cuba in 1962.

cases, the CIA must employ covert methods to uncover foreign secrets that could be vital to U.S. national security.

The CIA uses three major types of covert intelligence. The first is photographic intelligence, known as PHOTINT. Although PHOTINT involves all types of photographic information, its most important mission is overhead reconnaissance. PHOTINT uses high-altitude spy planes and satellites to photograph military installations, weapons depots, nuclear missile sites, and other strategic locations.

Although PHOTINT officially falls under the jurisdiction of the National Intelligence Tasking Center, other CIA departments take part in photographic intelligence as well. The Operations Directorate's Office of Imagery Analysis and the Science and Technology Directorate's National Photographic Interpretation Center each have a hand in evaluating photographic intelligence.

The Committee on Imagery Requirements and Exploitation (COMIREX)—comprising representatives from each of the intelligence agencies—oversees photographic intelligence.

Another covert intelligence method is signals intelligence, or SIGINT. Signals intelligence refers to the interception of radio, telephone, telegraph, and other forms of communication through such covert means as satellite interference and wiretapping. It also includes the monitoring of military communications, such as ship-to-shore phones and pilot-to-ground transmissions.

The CIA's SIGINT operations fall under the Directorate of Science and Technology and the National Intelligence Tasking Center. The intelligence arms of the army, navy, air force, and marines also gather signals intelligence. The SIGINT Committee, an oversight board similar to COMIREX and consisting of representatives of each intelligence branch, supervises signals intelligence operations.

Perhaps the most intriguing intelligence method is human intelligence, or HUMINT. As its name implies, human intelligence requires the use of people to gather information. Officers travel "under cover" to learn things that technical means cannot provide. Although recent advances in photographic and signals intelligence have somewhat reduced the need for human intelligence operations, HUMINT remains an important part of the CIA.

Unlike civilians who are debriefed after a foreign trip, HUMINT officers travel abroad with the intention of gathering intelligence. They pose as diplomats, scientists, travelers, or businesspeople. Government employees such as ambassadors and military personnel, who are not part of the intelligence community, also make significant contributions to HUMINT operations as part of their jobs.

Some HUMINT officers are not CIA employees at all, but ordinary people recruited because they have access to important information. Many are not even American citizens, but foreigners

To intercept electronic communications in foreign countries, the CIA uses space satellites like the one pictured here.

hired to spy within their own countries. Foreign HUMINT officers may work for an important corporation or for a branch of their government. Their work is the most dangerous method of intelligence collection, because they are completely at the mercy of their home government if their actions are discovered. For example, in October 1986, the Soviet Union executed scientist Adolf G. Tolkachev for allegedly supplying the CIA with information on stealth technology (the science of concealing aircraft and missiles from radar).

Covert Action: The Debate

The most controversial issue surrounding the CIA is its participation in covert operations, which take a number of forms. Primarily directed against the Soviet Union and its Communist satellite states, covert operations are usually small-scale actions. For example, the agency may fund a secret, anti-Communist radio station or newspaper in a Soviet-bloc country. Or it may work to develop labor unions or opposition political parties in unfriendly nations.

Some covert operations, however, are much more dangerous and sometimes employ paramilitary tactics. The CIA gives military aid to friendly governments and groups trying to overthrow unfriendly or Soviet-backed governments. It intercedes in wars in which the United States has an interest but does not want to become directly involved. It sometimes works to destabilize unfriendly governments by creating unrest in their countries.

The most well-known examples of these covert tactics occurred in the early 1960s, when Cuba, located not far from the coast of Florida, allied itself with the Soviet Union and began a military buildup. One plan, Operation MONGOOSE, was intended to undermine the Cuban economy by sabotaging factories and transportation systems and destroying Cuban exports. President Kennedy authorized this operation, although he rejected several of its specific plans, including a scheme to contaminate a shipload of Cuban sugar headed for the Soviet Union.

During the same period, separate plans focused on ways to assassinate Cuba's premier, Fidel Castro. In one scheme, the CIA intended to hire organized crime figures to kill Castro, theorizing that no one would suspect the CIA if the crime looked like a gangland slaying. Another reported plan involved offering Castro an exploding cigar when he visited the United Nations. A police inspector assigned to protect Castro during his visit claimed that a CIA officer confessed that the agency had planned to leave a "gift box" of Castro's favorite cigars in his hotel room but had abandoned the idea as too dangerous. The agency denied the story, although it admitted it once considered assassinating Castro. (Officials claim that the CIA now forbids assassination planning.) In the past, these and other reports brought the agency under fire.

More recently, the CIA's covert actions in Central America caused controversy. In April 1984, newspaper accounts revealed that the agency—without consulting Congress—had mined harbors in Nicaragua in an effort to aid the Contra rebels fighting Nicaragua's Communist Sandinista government. Later that year, six CIA officials admitted that they had written a manual on "neutralizing" officials of Nicaragua's unfriendly government. In October 1986, American Eugene Hasenfus was captured in Nicara-

The CIA conceived several schemes for assassinating Cuban premier Fidel Castro, including a plan to give him exploding cigars.

Sandinistas arrest Eugene Hasenfus in Nicaragua after shooting down his plane, which allegedly carried supplies for the Contras.

gua after the military supply plane in which he was flying was shot down. Hasenfus claimed he thought he was working for the CIA. And in early 1987, House and Senate committees began investigating alleged CIA involvement in channeling funds to Nicaragua's Contras at a time when this action was specifically forbidden by law.

Although the CIA denied involvement in many of these incidents, each episode caused public furor and renewed the national debate on the agency's role. CIA supporters contend that the National Security Act permits the agency to perform covert operations if so directed by the president and the NSC. Others claim that covert actions violate the tenets of democratic government by allowing the president to circumvent Congress and engage in undeclared wars. The controversy over these CIA activities has raged since the 1960s and seems likely to continue as the agency remains involved in covert action.

At CIA headquarters, a statue of espionage hero Nathan Hale stands as a reminder of America's long intelligence tradition.

SEVEN

American Intelligence: Then and Now

Nationl intelligence operations have changed dramatically since Nathan Hale spied on the British during the American Revolution. Acting alone, Hale relied on his eyes and ears to gather information on enemy troop movements. Today, about 16,000 CIA officers use computers, listening devices, and photographic techniques to gather data on everything from the Chinese economy to Soviet nuclear capabilities.

During the six years of the American Revolution, George Washington spent a total of $17,000 on secret intelligence, primarily to pay a few informants' salaries. Today, the intelligence community spends more than $24 billion every year on everything from spy planes to stationery. In Washington's time—and for years afterward—the United States used intelligence operations only against wartime enemies. When the fighting stopped, it dismantled these operations. Contemporary CIA officers work during war and peace to gather information on hostile and friendly governments alike in order to maintain national security.

World War II taught the United States that accurate intelligence is a vital survival tool in the 20th century.

These changes came about gradually, in response to a shift in America's view of its place in the world. Until the 1900s, the United States was politically isolated. It fought the revolutionary war and the Civil War on American soil for American political aims. But World War I and World War II brought the country into the forefront of world politics. As the new political, economic, and military leader of the Western nations, the United States could no longer afford to turn a blind eye toward events in other parts of the globe.

America's early leaders knew who their enemies were and what they were fighting against. In the 20th century, the bombing of Pearl Harbor—one of history's greatest intelligence failures—proved that things were no longer so clear-cut. The congressmen who created the CIA in 1947 responded to the realities of a shrinking world in which the politics of one nation inevitably affect many others.

Like the nation's intelligence needs, the CIA itself has changed since its creation. During the 1950s and 1960s, the fledgling agency grew rapidly as the cold war escalated and the United States and the Soviet Union became polarized. In the 1970s, revelations of wrongdoing led to reforms that severely limited the agency's power. Later, the conservatism of the 1980s permitted the CIA to reassert its power.

Whatever the national mood toward intelligence, controversy has always surrounded the CIA. Today, despite the national trend toward supporting for intelligence activities, questions persist about the agency's motives and techniques. Other members of the intelligence community, most notably the Defense Department's intelligence arm, complain that the CIA's activities often conflict with their own. The DCI and other intelligence chiefs frequently disagree.

In addition, there continues to be friction between Congress and the CIA. The agency's need for secrecy often conflicts with Congress's mandate to supervise intelligence activities and ensure that the agency operates within its charter. Throughout the 1980s, Congress continued to protest the agency's refusal to turn over information. As one member of the House intelligence subcommittee complained, "If [DCI] Bill Casey were Paul Revere, he wouldn't have told us the redcoats were coming until it was in the papers."

Finally, the greatest controversy surrounding the agency continues to be the American public's right to know. Intelligence operations, by their very nature quite secretive, cannot easily be reconciled with democracy, founded on the principal of openness between government and the public. When the public is kept in the dark about CIA operations, it complains that the agency is functioning as a "secret government." By the same token, when intelligence operations are revealed publicly (most often by the watchful American press), the CIA complains that its operations and its agents are compromised. This conflict has raged since the CIA was created in 1947, and it seems likely to continue.

No one can predict what changes the coming years will bring to the CIA. Like its past, the agency's future depends upon many factors—world politics, U.S. leadership, and American public opinion. What is certain, however, is that the CIA will continue to play a vital role in U.S. foreign policy as the world heads toward the 21st century.

GLOSSARY

Agent – A person engaged in espionage activities for a foreign intelligence agency. (CIA employees are known as officers.)

Classified information – Data that a government withholds from the public in an attempt to preserve national security.

Cold war – Prolonged hostility between two nations over ideological differences that does not involve overt military action. (Most often used to describe the state of relations between the United States and the Soviet Union after World War II.)

Counterintelligence – Techniques used by an intelligence agency to protect its operations and agents from discovery or interference by enemy organizations.

Cryptography – Creating and breaking secret writing or codes.

Espionage – The act or art of gaining information through covert (secret) activity.

Estimates: Analyses of "raw" intelligence issued by teams of CIA experts in the form of reports, bulletins, and surveys.

Intelligence – Information concerning an enemy or possible enemy.

Intelligence community – Those governmental agencies that have as at least part of their function the responsibility for gathering intelligence.

Paramilitary operations: limited military operations carried out by organizations whose functions are otherwise nonmilitary.

Signals intelligence – Intelligence acquired by intercepting electronic comunications.

Surveillance – Secret observation of a person or group.

SELECTED REFERENCES

Cline, Ray S. *The CIA: Under Reagan, Bush and Casey*. Washington, D.C.: Acropolis Books, 1981.

Colby, William. *Honorable Men: My Life in the CIA*. New York: Simon and Schuster, 1978.

Fain, Tyrus G., general ed. *The Intelligence Community: History, Organization, and Issues*. Public Documents Series. New York and London: R. R. Bowker Company, 1977.

Hymoff, Edward. *The OSS in World War II*. New York: Ballantine Books, 1972.

Kirkpatrick, Lyman B., Jr. *The Real CIA*. New York: Macmillan, 1968.

Leary, William M., ed. *The Central Intelligence Agency: History and Documents*. Tuscaloosa, AL: University of Alabama Press, 1984.

Oseth, John M. *Regulating U.S. Intelligence Operations: A Study in Definition of the National Interest*. Lexington, KY: University of Kentucky Press, 1985.

Powers, Thomas. *The Man Who Kept the Secrets*. New York: Knopf, 1979.

Tully, Andrew. *CIA: The Inside Story*. New York: William Morrow, 1962.

Wise, David and Thomas B. Ross. *The Espionage Establishment*. New York: Random House, 1967.

INDEX

N

National Foreign Intelligence
  Board (NFIB), 62, 74
National Intelligence Daily, 76
National Security Act of 1947, 18,
  36–37, 49, 59, 83
National Security Council (NSC),
  37, 53, 68–69, 75
Nicaragua, 57, 82
Nixon, Richard M., 45, 49

O

Office of Management and Budget
  (OMB), 70
Office of Naval Intelligence
  (ONI), 23
Office of Strategic Services
  (OSS), 29, 30–31, 35, 38, 40,
  44, 56
Operation CHAOS, 49
Operation MONGOOSE, 81

P

Pearl Harbor, 18, 28, 86
Pike, Otis, 50
Pike Committee, 51
Pinkerton, Allan, 20–21
Powers, Francis Gary, 41
Privacy Act of 1974, 71

R

Raborn, William, 43–44
Reagan, Ronald, 48, 55–56
Rockefeller, Nelson A., 48
Rockefeller Commission, 48, 49,
  50, 51
Roosevelt, Franklin D., 27, 28,
  30, 33, 35
Roosevelt, James, 28

S

Sandinistas (Nicaraguan leaders),
  82
Savoldi, Joe, 32
Schlesinger, James, 45, 47

Secret Intelligence Service (SIS), 29
Senate U.S., 52, 61, 69, 83
Senate Select Committee to
  Study Governmental
  Operations with Respect to
  Intelligence Activities, 50
Sharpe, George, 21
Smith, Walter Beddell, 38
Soviet Union, 17, 25, 35, 38, 41,
  42, 49, 51, 54, 57, 62, 80, 81
Spanish-American War, 23
Stalin, Josef, 35
State Department, U.S., 24, 28,
  69
Stephenson, William, 30
Stimson, Henry L., 26
Strong, George V., 28

T

Tallmadge, Benjamin, 20
Tolkachev, Adolf G., 80
Trujillo, Rafael, 51
Truman, Harry S., 33, 35, 36
Turner, Stansfield, 54

U

U-2 incident, 41
Union army, 20, 21
United Nations, 52
U.S. Navy, 23

V

Vietnam War, 43, 44–45, 54

W

Washington, George, 19, 20, 85
Watergate scandal, 45, 54
World War I, 24, 25, 27, 86
World War II, 18, 27, 28, 29, 33,
  38, 56, 86

Y

Yardley, Herbert O., 24, 25

Z

Zaire, 51

Rafaela Ellis, a Philadelphia-based writer and editor, holds a Master of Arts degree from Villanova University. Formerly an editorial researcher with the Augustinian Historical Institute, she currently works as an editor for an educational publisher.

Arthur M. Schlesinger, jr., served in the White House as special assistant to Presidents Kennedy and Johnson. He is the author of numerous acclaimed works in American history and has twice been awarded the Pulitzer Prize. He taught history at Harvard University for many years and is currently Albert Schweitzer Professor of the Humanities at the City University of New York.